H₂O damage - 6/1/10

P9-BIW-797

MOTHS

NIGHTTIME ANIMALS

Lynn M. Stone

The Rourke Corporation, Inc.
Vero Beach, Florida 32964

Edited by Sandra A. Robinson

PHOTO CREDITS
All photos © Lynn M. Stone

Library of Congress Cataloging-in-Publication Data

Stone, Lynn M.
    Moths / by Lynn M. Stone.
       p. cm. — (Nighttime animals)
    Includes index.
    Summary: Provides a detailed description of the life cycle and
habits of moths, as well as information on the variety of species
that exist and their general usefulness to man.
    ISBN 0-86593-297-2
    1. Moths—Juvenile literature. [1. Moths.] I. Title. II. Series:
Stone, Lynn M. Nighttime animals.
QL544.2.S785   1993
595.78'1—dc20
                                   93-15695
                                       CIP
                                        AC

TABLE OF CONTENTS

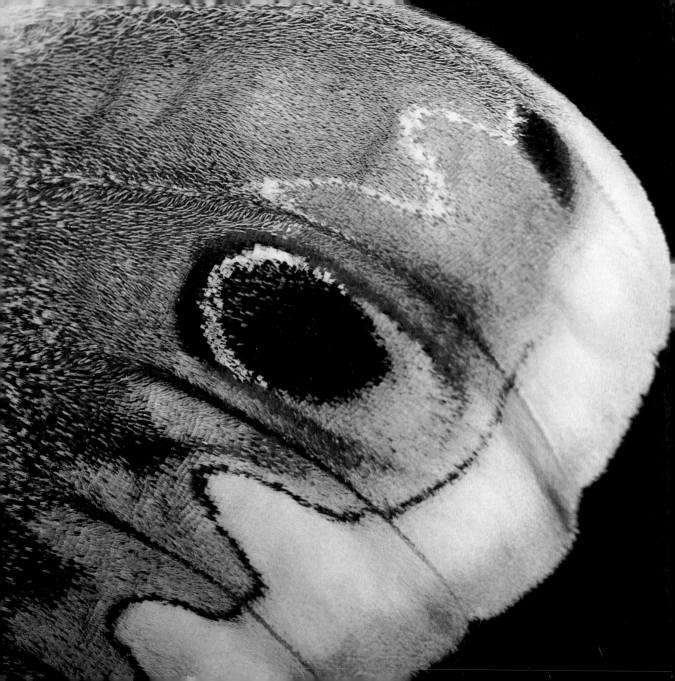

MOTHS

Moths are flying insects closely related to butterflies. Butterflies, however, are active in daylight. Most moths are **nocturnal**—active at night.

Because moths fly in darkness, most people do not realize that many **species,** or kinds, of moths have wings as brightly-colored as butterflies. Like butterfly wings, moth wings are covered by thousands of tiny scales.

Some species of moths are less than an inch across their open wings. The largest moths have a 12-inch wingspan.

Thousands of tiny, colorful scales cover the wings of most moths

KINDS OF MOTHS

Thousands of moth species live throughout the world. Hundreds of species live in North America.

Some of the best-known groups of moths in North America are the giant silk moths, tiger moths, hawk moths, owlet moths and measuring-worm moths.

Many of the large moths have colorful, round markings or see-through spots on their wings. These are called "eyespots" because they look like eyes. They may scare the moth's enemies.

One of the giant silk moths, a polyphemus, shows off its "eyespots"

MOTH COUSINS

Together, moths and butterflies make up a group of more than 100,000 species of insects. Moths and butterflies are alike in many ways.

Generally, you can tell a moth from a butterfly by when it flies—during the night or day. Also, a moth's two antennas are usually feathery. Moths usually have shorter, fatter bodies than butterflies, and they land with their wings spread. Butterflies usually land with wings raised.

Feathery antennas and a thick body help separate moths from butterflies

FROM EGG TO ADULT

The moth's life has four stages—egg, **larva, pupa** and adult. The larva is the caterpillar that hatches from the egg. Many moth caterpillars look quite strange. They may have "horns," bristles, knobs and humps as defenses against **predators,** the animals that would like to eat them. The touch of some prickly caterpillars irritates human skin.

Several moth caterpillars spin a **cocoon,** a little envelope, of silk. The caterpillar stays in the cocoon as a pupa, the resting stage of moth life. Later an adult moth comes out of the cocoon.

A cecropia moth lays its eggs from an opening at the lower end of its body

The silken cocoon of a cecropia, North America's largest moth

The Io moth caterpillar is a crawling cushion of "pins"

WHAT MOTHS EAT

Most moth caterpillars eat plants. Adult moths live on liquids—or on food stored in their bodies.

Adult moths that feed have a **proboscis**—a long, strawlike tube that reaches from their mouth. A moth sticks the proboscis into a flower's pool of sweet **nectar** and sucks it into its mouth.

Several species of adult moths, such as the cecropia, don't eat—they live on their body fat. They live just a few days as adults.

The hummingbird moth feeds on a milkweed flower

WHERE MOTHS LIVE

North American moths live in many different places, including deserts, forests, gardens and meadows. Some even live in the cold Far North.

A moth species must live where its food plants live. Each species of moth will eat only certain plants. A cecropia moth, for example, lives only in the eastern half of North America. That is where its food plants grow.

A cecropia lays its eggs near a food plant that the cecropia caterpillar will munch

MOTH HABITS

Some moths have an amazing sense of smell. A male cecropia moth's antennas can find the scent of a female cecropia that is one mile away!

To escape daytime predators, many moths have natural **camouflage.** Their colors blend with their surroundings. Some moths look like tree bark.

At night, however, certain kinds of owls, bats and spiders catch moths.

The antennas of a male cecropia can smell a distant female

GIANT SILK MOTHS

The largest and most colorful moths in North America are the giant silk moths. Thirteen hundred species of giant silk moths live world-wide. Among the North American species are the cecropia, cynthia, polyphemus, promethea, Io and the beautiful, lime green luna.

Giant silk moth caterpillars spin cocoons of threadlike silk strands. Some species wrap leaves into their cocoons, too.

Air pollution, which has damaged trees and their leaves, is one reason that many of these large moths have disappeared.

Trailing wing tails help identify the lime green luna moth

MOTHS AND PEOPLE

Moths are an important part of nature. They provide food for many predators. They help plants grow by spreading **pollen** from one plant to another. Pollen is used by plants in reproduction.

In Asia, silk moths produce strands of silk for cloth. One strand may be three-quarters of a mile long!

Some moths are harmful to the interests of people. Moth caterpillars damage crops, trees and even clothes.

Glossary

camouflage (KAM o flahj) — to hide by matching an animal's color to its surroundings

cocoon (KUH koon) — the covering—often of silk—in which a moth pupa rests and sometimes spends the winter

larva (LAR vuh) — the state of insect development between egg and pupa

nectar (NEK ter) — a sweet liquid made by flowers

nocturnal (nahk TUR nul) — active at night

predator (PRED uh tor) — an animal that kills other animals for food

pollen (PAHL in) — dustlike grains produced by flowers and necessary for flower reproduction

proboscis (pro BAH sis) — the long, coiled feeding tube of butterflies and moths

pupa (PYU puh) — the stage of development between larva and adult when the insect is inactive

species (SPEE sheez) — within a group of closely-related living things, one certain kind or type (*cecropia* moth)

INDEX